Glaciers

WITHDRAWN

by Colleen Sexton

BELLWETHER MEDIA • MINNEAPOLIS, MN

Note to Librarians, Teachers, and Parents:

Blastoff! Readers are carefully developed by literacy experts and combine standards-based content with developmentally-appropriate text.

Level 1 provides the most support through repetition of high-frequency words, light text, predictable sentence patterns, and strong visual support.

Level 2 offers early readers a bit more challenge through varied simple sentences, increased text load, and less repetition of high frequency words.

Level 3 advances early-fluent readers toward fluency through increased text and concept load, less reliance on visuals, longer sentences, and more literary language.

Level 4 builds reading stamina by providing more text per page, increased use of punctuation, greater variation in sentence patterns, and increasingly challenging vocabulary.

Level 5 encourages children to move from "learning to read" to "reading to learn" by providing even more text, varied writing styles, and less familiar topics.

Whichever book is right for your reader, Blastoff! Readers are the perfect books to build confidence and encourage a love of reading that will last a lifetime!

This edition first published in 2008 by Bellwether Media.

No part of this publication may be reproduced in whole or in part without written permission of the publisher. For information regarding permission, write to Bellwether Media Inc., Attention: Permissions Department, Post Office Box 1C, Minnetonka, MN 55345-9998.

Library of Congress Cataloging-in-Publication Data
Sexton, Colleen A., 1967–
  Glaciers / by Colleen Sexton.
    p. cm. — (Blastoff! readers. Learning about the Earth)
Summary: "Simple text and supportive images introduce beginning readers to the physical characteristics and geographic locations of glaciers"–Provided by publisher.
  Includes bibliographical references and index.
  ISBN-13: 978-1-60014-113-3 (hardcover : alk. paper)
  ISBN-10: 1-60014-113-7 (hardcover : alk. paper)
  1. Glaciers—Juvenile literature. I. Title.

GB2403.8.S49 2008
551.31'2—dc22   2007017570

Contents

Glaciers are huge rivers of flowing ice and snow. Most glaciers are found in **Antarctica**.

Glaciers are also found on high mountain peaks in most parts of the world. These areas are covered by snow all year long.

Glaciers have three parts. The top layer is snow. The middle layer is a mix of snow and ice. The bottom layer is solid ice.

Glaciers form over thousands of years. They begin to form when snow falls and covers the land.

New snow falls
on top of the old
snow. The layers of
snow grow deeper
every year.

The bottom layers of snow pack down and turn into ice.

The ice grows thicker and thicker. It becomes heavy and starts to slide downhill. It spreads out as it moves.

The ice in a glacier can bend to flow over uneven ground. Glaciers can even turn around large rocks or cliffs.

Most glaciers move a few inches or a few feet each day. The fastest glaciers can move 100 feet (30 meters) in a day.

Fast moving glaciers can crack.
A crack in a glacier is called
a **crevasse**.

Glaciers grind away the earth as they move. They pick up rocks along the way.

Glaciers push the rocks to the sides making long hills called **moraines**.

Glaciers carve U-shaped valleys in the earth. Lakes form in these valleys.

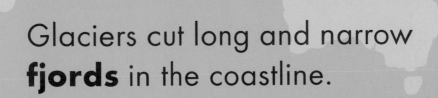

Glaciers cut long and narrow **fjords** in the coastline.

Some glaciers flow off the land and into the ocean. A thick block of ice called an ice shelf forms where the land meets the ocean.

ice shelf

iceberg

Waves crash against ice shelves. Huge chunks called **icebergs** break off and float away to sea.

Some glaciers melt when they reach warmer places. Streams of **meltwater** carve out tunnels and caves in the ice.

Meltwater also flows into rivers and lakes. People use this water to make power and water crops. They also drink it. Maybe you've used water that came from a glacier!

Glossary

Antarctica—the continent covering the South Pole

crevasse—a deep and narrow crack in the top of a glacier

fjord—a long and narrow bay cut into the coastline by a glacier; the sides of a fjord are very steep.

iceberg—a huge chunk of ice in the ocean; icebergs break off of glaciers.

meltwater—water from melting snow or ice

moraine—a mound of rocks, pebbles, sand, and mud formed by a glacier; moraines are often long ridges.

To Learn More

AT THE LIBRARY
Corral, Kimberly. *A Child's Glacier Bay*. Anchorage, Alaska: Northwest Books, 1998.

Fowler, Allan. *Icebergs, Ice Caps, and Glaciers*. New York: Children's Press, 1997.

Muir, John. *Stickeen: John Muir and the Brave Little Dog*. Nevada City, Calif.: Dawn Publications, 1998.

Simon, Seymour. *Icebergs and Glaciers*. New York: HarperTrophy, 1999.

ON THE WEB
Learning more about glaciers is as easy as 1, 2, 3.

1. Go to www.factsurfer.com

2. Enter "glaciers" into search box.

3. Click the "Surf" button and you will see a list of related web sites.

With factsurfer.com, finding more information is just a click away.

Index

The photographs in this book are reproduced through the courtesy of: Juan Martinez, front cover, pp. 8-9; Svetlana Privezentseva, p. 4; Remi Cauzid, p. 5; Gavin Hellier/Getty Images, pp. 6-7; PatitucciPhoto/Getty Images, pp. 10-11; Wes Walker/Getty Images, p. 12; Steve Bloom Images/Alamy, p. 13; David Sacks/Getty Images, pp. 14-15; Alan Kearney/Getty Images, p. 16; Pep Roig/Alamy, p. 17; Dea/Agarozzo/Getty Images, pp. 18-19; Fred Hirschmann//Getty Images, p. 20; Gavin Hellier/Robert Harding/Getty Images, p. 21.